The Science of Living Things

What is a Biome?

A Bobbie Kalman Book

Crabtree Publishing Company

www.crabtreebooks.com

The Science of Living Things Series
A Bobbie Kalman Book

For Susie Demers
whose smile is warmer than the Punta Cana sun

Author and Editor-in-Chief
Bobbie Kalman

Managing editor
Lynda Hale

Editors
Greg Nickles
Jacqueline Langille
April Fast

Text and photo research
April Fast

Computer design
Lynda Hale
McVannel Communications Inc.
(cover concept)

Production coordinator
Hannelore Sotzek

Crabtree Publishing Company
www.crabtreebooks.com   1-800-387-7650

Printed in the USA/012010/CG20091228

Cataloging in Publication Data
Kalman, Bobbie
    What is a biome?
(The science of living things)
Includes index.
ISBN 0-86505- 875-X (library bound)   ISBN 0-86505- 887-3 (pbk.)
This book introduces biomes, showing and describing the main kinds and
discussing their location, climate, and plant and animal life.

1. Biotic communities—Juvenile literature. [1. Biotic communities.] I. Title.
II.Series: Kalman, Bobbie. Science of living things.
QH541.14.K35 1997   j577   LC 97-39885
                                                        CIP

Published in
the United States
PMB 59051
350 Fifth Avenue,
59th Floor
New York, New York
10118

Published
in Canada
616 Welland Ave.,
St. Catharines,
Ontario, Canada
L2M 5V6

Published in the
United Kingdom
Maritime House
Basin Road North,
Hove
BN41 1WR
United Kingdom

Published
in Australia
386 Mt. Alexander Rd.,
Ascot Vale (Melbourne)
V1C 3032

Contents

What is a biome?

Biomes are huge natural areas on Earth where certain types of plants grow. The ocean biome, for example, is made up of all the oceans on Earth. The **climate**, type of soil, and animals are all part of a biome. There can be thousands of **ecosystems** within a biome. An ecosystem is the relationship between plants and animals in a smaller environment, such as a pond. Earth has over 30 types of biomes. This map shows some of Earth's major biomes.

- Forests
- Grasslands
- Shrub and scrublands
- Deserts
- Mountains
- Tundra

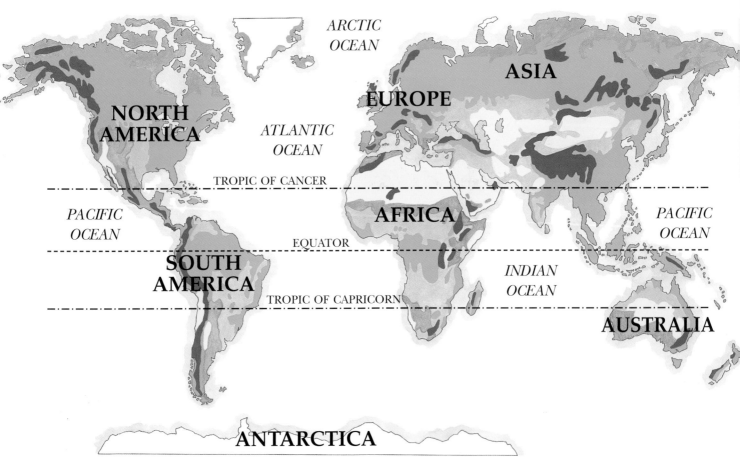

ARCTIC OCEAN

ASIA

EUROPE

NORTH AMERICA

ATLANTIC OCEAN

TROPIC OF CANCER

PACIFIC OCEAN

AFRICA

PACIFIC OCEAN

EQUATOR

SOUTH AMERICA

INDIAN OCEAN

TROPIC OF CAPRICORN

AUSTRALIA

ANTARCTICA

Blending naturally

Biomes blend naturally into one another. A **grassland** biome, for example, can end at the edge of a **forest** or in a **wetland**. Some animals **migrate** from one biome to another when the seasons change. Many birds visit several biomes in search of food or nesting areas.

Depending on one another

The plants and animals in a biome depend on one another for survival. Plants provide food and shelter for animals. Animals help spread the seeds of plants.

The flow of energy

All the living things in a biome need **energy** to live and grow. Energy comes from the sun and flows through all living things. The more daylight hours a biome has, the more sun energy its living things receive.

Food chains and webs

Plants trap the energy of the sun and use the **carbon dioxide** in air to make food. They are the only living things that can use sunlight to make food. Animals cannot make their own food because they cannot trap the sun's energy.

To get energy, animals must eat plants or other animals. Animals that eat other animals that eat plants form a **food chain**. Food chains that are linked together in a biome make up a **food web**.

This picture shows a simple food chain:
1. Energy comes from the sun.
2. Plants use sunlight to make food.
*3. **Herbivores**, such as rabbits, eat plants.*
*4. **Carnivores**, such as wolves, eat rabbits.*
5. Nutrients from the remains of dead plants and animals help new plants grow.

What is climate?

The plants and animals that live in a biome depend on its climate. Climate is the weather that an area has had over a long period of time, such as 30 years. Weather changes from day to day, but climate is the weather people expect. Rain or snow, temperature, wind, and sunlight are all part of climate. The location of a biome affects its climate. Being near the equator, North and South poles, high on a mountain, or near an ocean can affect the climate in a biome.

This map shows the areas of the Earth that are hot, mild, and cold.

- always hot
- always mild
- hot summer, mild winter
- hot summer, cool winter
- hot summer, cold winter
- mild summer, cool winter
- mild summer, cold winter
- cool summer, cold winter
- always cold

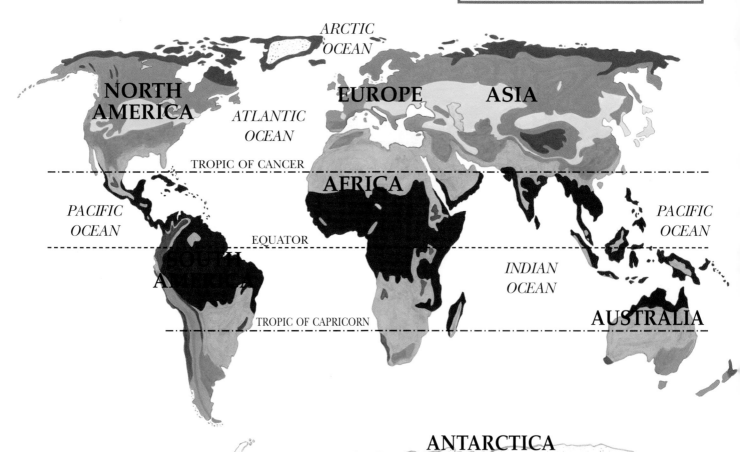

ARCTIC OCEAN

NORTH AMERICA

EUROPE   ASIA

ATLANTIC OCEAN

TROPIC OF CANCER

AFRICA

PACIFIC OCEAN

PACIFIC OCEAN

EQUATOR

INDIAN OCEAN

TROPIC OF CAPRICORN

AUSTRALIA

ANTARCTICA

Tropical biomes

Look at the map on page 6. Find the equator, tropic of Cancer, and tropic of Capricorn. Using the color legend above the map, describe the climate in this area. What did you discover? The climate in this region is called a **tropical** climate. In some tropical areas, the weather is the same every day. In others, there are rainy and dry seasons.

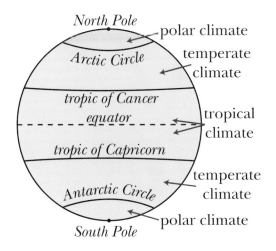

Polar areas

The regions near the North and South Poles, above and below the Arctic and Antarctic Circles, have a **polar** climate. Much of these areas are freezing cold and covered with ice all year. There is a short summer and a long, dark winter. Find the polar regions on the globe.

Temperate zones

Two **temperate** regions lie between the tropical and polar regions. Depending on their location, they have cold or cool winters and hot or warm summers. Some temperate areas have four seasons: winter, spring, summer, and fall. Others have wet and dry seasons. Find the temperate regions on the globe and map.

A biome that is near an ocean has a milder climate than one that is in the center of a continent because the temperature of water does not change very much. Land areas, on the other hand, heat up and cool down quickly.

Adapting to biomes

Plants and animals are well suited to the biome in which they live. Over time, plants **adapt**, or change, so they can get as much sunshine and water as possible for making food. Some **desert** plants have long roots for finding water deep in the soil. In areas where a lot of rain falls, many plants have wide, flat leaves. Water **evaporates** quickly off large leaves. In cold, dry areas, plants grow close to the soil so their stems will not be broken by strong winds.

(above) The hairs on the stems of arctic poppies help hold in water. They also keep the plants warm by trapping warm air around them. The colorful blossoms absorb more of the sun's rays than white flowers do.

(below) Some plants have adapted to living in wetland biomes by sending up large, flat leaves and flowers to the water's surface to catch sunlight. African jacanas have adapted to walking on these water plants. Their long toes spread their body weight over a large area so it does not cause the leaf to sink.

Animals also adapt

Some animals have bodies that are specially suited to their biome home. Animals that live in cold-climate biomes often have thick fur or a layer of fat to keep them warm. Many tropical animals have large ears that give off extra body heat and allow them to stay cool.

Some animals adapt to their biome by behaving in certain ways. Most desert animals sleep during the day to avoid the hot sun, but grassland herbivores graze in daylight in order to see **predators** approaching. Some animals adapt slowly over time, and others, such as the raccoon, adapt quickly. In less than one hundred years, raccoons have learned to live in cities.

Fennec foxes live in hot deserts, so they have large ears to give off extra body heat.

The red foxes that live in temperate meadows have medium-sized ears to let some body heat escape in warm weather.

The arctic fox, found in the far north, has small ears to keep its body heat from escaping.

The fur on the soles of a polar bear's feet stops it from slipping on ice. The bear's thick, white coat keeps it warm and helps it blend in with snow and ice.

Rainforest trees are slippery because of the moist climate of this biome. Tree frogs have long toes with sticky tips to help them climb the wet trees.

Forest biomes

Forest biomes are filled with large trees and other, smaller plants. Forests are very important to the Earth. They use up large amounts of carbon dioxide to make their food. Carbon dioxide is a gas that is dangerous to people and animals when there is too much of it in the air. Forests also freshen the air by releasing **oxygen** through their leaves. Oxygen is a gas that people and animals need to breathe. Forest biomes can be found in cold, tropical, and temperate areas.

Boreal forests

Boreal forests, also known as **taiga,** are located in northern areas of the world and near the tops of high mountains. They have long, dry, cold winters and short, warm summers. In winter, thick snow covers the ground. It acts as a blanket and prevents the ground from freezing.

Conifers, or trees with cones, grow in boreal forests. These trees are also called **evergreens** because their leaves stay green year round. Bushes, shrubs, ferns, and mosses also grow in boreal forests.

The thin, waxy needles of conifers hold in water and shed snow easily so the branches will not break from its weight. Their seeds are contained in cones.

Taiga animals

Carnivores, including weasels, mink, wolves, wolverines, owls, and hawks, hunt in the taiga. Some animals, such as deer and squirrels, live in the taiga all year, and others, such as caribou, live there only in winter. Bears rest in caves or burrows during the winter and hunt for food in the forest all summer.

Herbivores such as deer find plenty of food during summer in the taiga.

Temperate forests

Temperate areas have warm, wet summers and cool winters. Several types of forests grow in this climate. Some forest biomes have a warmer climate and more rain than others.

Temperate rainforests

Temperate rainforests receive a rainfall of 80 inches (203 cm) a year. Both **broad-leaved** trees and conifers grow in these biomes. Broad-leaved trees have wide leaves instead of needles. Ferns, bushes, and flowers also grow in the temperate rainforest.

*Spotted owls and other birds are becoming **endangered** because they need to live in old trees with holes, and the temperate rainforests that contain these trees are being cut down for lumber.*

The trees in temperate rainforests are among the tallest in the world. Huge conifers such as these redwoods in northern California grow to a height of

300 feet (91 m)! Sunlight and rain reach the forest floor, so many small plants such as ferns and flowering plants are able to grow there.

Deciduous forests

Temperate **deciduous** forests have trees with broad leaves. These trees do not make food during winter because there is not enough rain or sunshine. Their leaves turn color and fall. In the colder, northern regions, conifers grow among the deciduous trees. A forest with these two types of trees is called a **mixed forest**.

Home to many animals

Temperate forests are alive with animal life! Birds and squirrels build their nests among the branches and in tree holes. Insects feed off the leaves and bark. On the forest floor, rabbits live in tunnels, and foxes make their homes in dens. Frogs and snakes live among the fallen leaves, branches, and tree roots.

Foxes live in dens in the roots of old trees or in other hidden spots on the forest floor.

emergents

canopy

understory

forest floor

Tropical rainforests

Tropical rainforests are found near the equator, between the tropic of Cancer and the tropic of Capricorn, where there is little change in the weather throughout the year. It is always hot. Tropical rainforests receive 60 to 160 inches (150-406 cm) of rain each year. Although they cover less than one-fifth of the Earth's land, they support over a million-and-a-half **species**, or types, of animals and plants.

Three levels of the forest

A tropical rainforest has three main levels: the **canopy** is the top layer that covers most of the forest, the **understory** is the middle layer, and the forest floor is the bottom layer. Each layer is home to many animals. Insects live in every layer.

The fruits and leaves of the canopy provide food for birds, bats, squirrels, and monkeys. Giant trees called **emergents** poke through the top of the canopy.

A layer of small, shade-loving trees, bushes, and vines, grows in the understory. Snakes, ocelots, tree frogs, and some birds such as guans live in this layer.

Tapirs and other herbivores live on the forest floor, which receives little sunlight. These animals are hunted by predators such as jaguars and snakes.

The golden lion tamarin is a monkey that lives in Brazil's coastal rainforest. The leafy canopy shades the monkey from the sun. Golden lion tamarins have long fingers and claws for gripping tree branches. This type of monkey is in danger of losing its home because much of the rainforest has been cut down to make room for farming.

Shrub and scrublands

Shrub and **scrubland** biomes are found in dry, temperate areas. They have mild winters and very hot summers. Dry weather and lightning storms sometimes cause **flash fires** during summer.

Flash fires start and spread quickly. They make room for new plants to grow by burning the large, older plants. The heat of the fire causes seed shells to crack. After the fire, the seeds sprout and grow into new plants.

Hardy plants

Low-growing, woody plants with evergreen leaves are the main type of vegetation in this biome. These plants have leaves with a tough skin that holds in moisture, and thorns that protect the plants from grazing animals. Many plants have long roots that enable them to find water underground. Some suck water from the stems of other plants.

*(below) Kudus feed on the leaves of a **scrub forest** in eastern Africa. Scrub forests can be found on the edges of grasslands. Short, thorny trees grow in these forests.*

*(above) The scrublands of California and Arizona are called **chaparral**. The chaparral is covered with small bushes.*

saguaro cactus

Deserts

Deserts are biomes that receive less than ten inches (25 cm) of rainfall or other types of **precipitation** a year. Deserts are not always hot, sandy places. There are also cold deserts.

Some deserts are huge areas of sand where plants cannot grow. Others are bare patches of rock. A few, however, such as the Sonoran desert in the southwest United States, are home to many types of plants. Most of the plants in this biome are **succulents**. They have thick, waxy skin and needles for holding in water. The saguaro cactus is a succulent that stores water in its stem.

Very few plants can grow in sandy deserts.

After it rains, many desert grasses burst into bloom, but the flowers quickly die.

Coping with heat and drought

Hot deserts receive little rainfall and a lot of sunshine. The animals that live there have found ways to cope.

Kangaroo rats waste very little water in their urine because it is almost dry.

Rattlesnakes hunt only at night during the hot summer months.

The prickly pear makes a juicy meal for animals that can get past its sharp needles. This peccary can!

Jackrabbits lose extra body heat through their large ears. To get water, they eat succulents such as cacti.

Camels store fat in their humps. During dry spells, their bodies break down the fat to get water.

Reptiles, such as this desert tortoise, have waterproof skin. They lose very little water through it.

The prairie dog stays cool in its underground burrow during the day and looks for food at night.

Grasslands

Grassland biomes are covered with grass, shrubs, and a few trees. Most types of trees cannot grow in grassland biomes because there is not enough rain. Natural fires that occur in grasslands kill trees, but they do not kill the grasses.

Prairies, plains, and meadows are temperate grassland biomes that receive between 10 and 20 inches (25-50 cm) of rain each year. They support hundreds of types of insects, birds, and animals. The picture below shows a meadow and prairie.

The savannah

The tropical grassland biome is called the **savannah**. It is hot and dry for more than half the year. During the dry season, the grass turns brown and dies. Sometimes fires burn the grass. When it rains, its deep roots sprout again, and the grass grows tall.

The animals of the grasslands

Some of the largest animals in the world live in the savannah. Herbivores such as elephants, giraffes, and wildebeests feed on grasses, small shrubs, and trees. They travel from one area to another in search of new plants to eat. Savannah herbivores are hunted by predators such as lions, cheetahs, leopards, and hyenas.

Many types of kangaroos live on the grasslands of Australia and New Zealand.

Predators find plenty of food in the savannah biome. This female lion is about to catch a wart hog for dinner.

The arctic tundra

The land just below the northern ice cap is called the arctic **tundra**. This biome is a cold desert—very little snow or rain falls there. During part of the winter, the sun never rises, and during part of the summer, it never sets.

Hardy plants

Only small, strong plants are able to survive in the Arctic. Larger plants such as trees cannot grow because the soil beneath the surface of the tundra is always frozen. This frozen ground is called **permafrost**. Arctic plants include lichens, mosses, sedges, and some flowering plants. Hardy tundra plants grow close to the ground, where they find protection from cold winds.

The saxifrage grows in a low, tight cushion in order to trap the sun's heat. It sends out shoots to start new plants. Its buds can live through the winter and bloom in the spring.

The rhododendron has waxy leaves that prevent water loss. The dark, cup-shaped flowers direct sunlight toward the flower's center, where its seeds grow.

lichen

moss

Mosses and lichens grow on the surface of rocks. Rocks help keep plants warm by sheltering them from the wind.

Adapting to the cold

Arctic animals have adapted to the cold tundra winters. Sea mammals such as seals and walruses have thick layers of **blubber**, or fat, to keep them warm. Land mammals often have thick fur coats. Ground squirrels and lemmings **hibernate**, or become inactive, during the winter.

Arctic summers

In summer, insects thrive on the tundra, which is dotted with ponds. Birds migrate to the Arctic to enjoy the insects and long summer days. Many animals, such as caribou, also migrate to the tundra in summer. Polar bears, arctic foxes, snowshoe hares, and musk oxen stay all year.

Animals such as the arctic fox change color to blend in with the snow. They have two layers of fur to keep them warm.

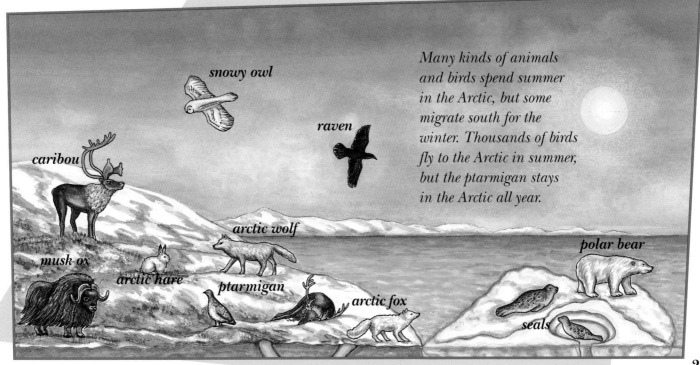

Many kinds of animals and birds spend summer in the Arctic, but some migrate south for the winter. Thousands of birds fly to the Arctic in summer, but the ptarmigan stays in the Arctic all year.

snowy owl

raven

caribou

arctic wolf

polar bear

musk ox

arctic hare

ptarmigan

arctic fox

seals

Wetlands

Bogs, swamps, and marshes are wetland biomes. All wetland biomes have waterlogged soil. Bogs and swamps are always flooded, but a marsh is wet only part of the year. Some wetlands are flooded with salty ocean water. Others are covered with fresh water from rivers and lakes.

Where is it wet?

Wetland biomes are found all over the world. They are often near lakes and rivers, but they also develop in sunken areas of grassy plains. All wetlands are important wildlife areas. Millions of plants and animals make wetlands their full- or part-time homes.

Wetland plants

Grasses, reeds, mosses, and evergreen trees grow in wetlands. Most of these plants grow only in certain climates, but sedges grow in all wetlands. One very important plant is the water hyacinth. It helps remove pollution from water.

sedge   *water hyacinth*

Pitcher plants grow only in wetlands. They are like slippery jugs filled with liquid. Insects slip down the side of the leaf, and the plant's juices turn them into liquid food.

Important to animals

Wetlands are important biomes for many types of animal life. Millions of birds make temporary homes in the wetlands in order to raise babies. Fish and shellfish lay eggs that hatch among the roots of plants. Snakes, turtles, frogs, raccoons, and salamanders can find plenty of food in the wetlands.

One of the few remaining natural homes for alligators is the Everglades, a large wetland biome in Florida. It is a national park, where thousands of types of birds and animals are protected, including herons, alligators, and snakes. In the Everglades there are tall grasses, channels of water, and areas of large cypress trees.

(inset) Raccoons live throughout the wetlands on dry land and in the trees.

Freshwater biomes

Freshwater biomes are filled with water that is not salty. There are two kinds of freshwater biomes. Rivers and streams have moving water. Lakes and ponds have slow-moving or still water. Less wildlife grows in rivers and streams because it is washed away by the **current**, or movement, of the water.

Some freshwater animals have adapted to living in rivers so they are not carried away by the current. Fish always swim upstream. Other creatures hold onto rocks using suckers or slime.

Freshwater plants

Underwater plants need to stay close to the water's surface so sunlight can reach them. Some freshwater plants, such as water lilies, grow flowers and leaves that float on the water's surface.

Fast-moving river water often pours into lakes, bringing fresh water to the plants and animals that live in the slow-moving lake water.

Pond life

Like a lake, a pond has still water. Many types of plants and animals live in ponds because they are not in danger of being swept away by a current. No two ponds have exactly the same plants and animals, but water lilies grow in almost every one. Most pond animals spend their time looking for food.

In the pond shown below, insects, birds, and small fish eat the water plants. Frogs eat the insects, and large fish eat the small fish. Large birds and snapping turtles eat the tadpoles, frogs, and fish.

Oceans

The oceans and seas form the **marine** biome, the world's largest biome. It covers three-quarters of the Earth and reaches from the far north to the far south of the planet. Oceans are filled with salt water. Their climate stays the same year round, so the creatures of the sea do not have to adapt to changing seasons.

Marine plants

Ocean water is filled with nutrients that plants need to stay alive. Most marine creatures depend on plants called **algae** as their main food. Very small types of algae are called **phytoplankton**. Phytoplankton floats through the water. Other ocean plants include sea grasses and seaweed called kelp.

Ocean animals

All types of creatures live in the oceans. **Zooplankton** are the tiniest animals. They float through the water and feed on phytoplankton. **Nekton** are animals that move around by swimming. Many types of nekton, including fish, whales, and rays, are found in every level of the ocean.

Sponges, crabs, and whales

Some ocean animals such as sponges and anemones are attached to one place all their life. These animals grab or suck in their food as it passes by on the ocean current. Lobsters, crabs, and other **crustaceans** live on the sea bottom. The ocean is also home to many mammals, from seals and sea lions to dolphins and whales.

oystercatcher

curlew

plover

avocet

spoonbill

sandpiper

(above) Coral reefs are known as the rainforests of the sea. More types of undersea creatures live in coral reefs than anywhere else in the ocean.

(opposite) On muddy and sandy beaches, shore birds dig clams, crabs, and tiny crustaceans from the mud for food.

(below) The coasts of oceans are separate biomes. There are rocky, sandy, stony, and muddy coasts. Rocky coasts often have tide pools, or areas where water is trapped when the tide goes out. Heat from sunlight warms the tide pools until the tide returns. These warm pools are filled with wildlife such as seaweed, sponges, sea stars, and minnows.

A TIDE POOL
AT LOW TIDE

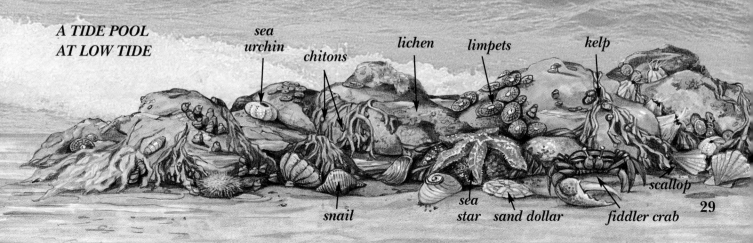

sea urchin

chitons

lichen

limpets

kelp

snail

sea star

sand dollar

fiddler crab

scallop

29

Biomes in danger

Forests

People burn and clear trees for timber, firewood, and to make way for farmland, mines, roads, and houses. When the trees are cleared, forests and their wildlife disappear. Mines and mills also pollute forest land.

Shrub and scrubland

When people build houses and settle in shrub and scrublands, they hunt the wildlife or push it out of its home. Humans cut down the trees for timber or fuel and allow their cattle and goats to eat all the natural plants.

Deserts

People pump water from underground sources to provide moisture for farming in the desert. The natural plants and animals lose their home to the farms. The water supplies are drained, so the desert becomes even drier.

Grasslands

Humans farm the grasslands and replace grasses with crops such as wheat. Their cattle graze on the remaining grass. New plants will not grow because farming takes important nutrients from the soil.

The arctic tundra

People damage the tundra by driving over it and throwing garbage on it. Tire tracks on the land take fifty years to go away, and garbage poisons the plants and animals. Polluted air from southern cities kills arctic plants.

Wetlands

Humans often put wetlands out of balance. Pesticides from farms and pollution from towns and cities wash into wetlands and damage wildlife. Wetlands disappear when they are drained to build new houses.

Freshwater biomes

Humans use water from rivers and lakes to cool machines in power stations and factories. When they release the water back into the river, it is warm. Warm water does not hold enough oxygen to keep plants and animals alive.

Oceans

When people catch too many fish, birds, dolphins, and other fish-eaters cannot find enough food. Drilling for oil in the ocean also causes problems. The rigs often spill oil into the water. The oil makes plants and animals sick.

Words to know

algae Green plants that grow in water and do not have roots, stems, or leaves

biome A large natural area that contains certain types of plants and animals

carbon dioxide A gas, made up of carbon and oxygen, that is present in air

carnivore An animal that eats other animals

conifer A tree that has needles and cones instead of leaves; also called evergreen

crustacean A creature, such as a crab, that has a shell and jointed limbs, or legs

deciduous Describing a forest with trees that lose their leaves before winter

desert A dry area with few plants and extremely hot or cold temperatures

endangered Describing a living thing that is in danger of becoming extinct

energy The power needed to do things

evaporate To change a liquid, such as water, into a vapor, or mist

extinct Describing a plant or animal that no longer exists

food web Two or more food chains that connect when a member of one food chain eats a member of another food chain

grassland An area that is covered mainly with grass and shrubs

herbivore An animal that eats mainly plants

hibernate To be asleep or inactive for a long period of time; some animals hibernate during the cold winter months

migrate To move to another area temporarily

mixed forest A forest that has both conifers and deciduous trees

nekton All creatures that swim—from tiny organisms to huge whales

omnivore An animal that eats both plants and animals

oxygen A gas present in air that humans, animals, and plants need to breathe

permafrost A layer of permanently frozen soil that is beneath the top layer of soil

phytoplankton Tiny plants that grow in water

polar Describing the freezing-cold climate of the arctic regions

precipitation Water, such as rain, snow, or hail, that falls to the Earth's surface

predator An animal that preys on, or hunts, other animals

savannah A broad, flat grassland found in tropical areas

shrub or **scrubland** A dry area that has stunted, or poorly grown, plants

temperate Describing a climate that is neither too hot nor too cold

tropic of Cancer The northern boundary of the tropical zone

tropic of Capricorn The southern boundary of the tropical zone

tropical Describing a hot, wet climate

wetland An area that has waterlogged soil

zooplankton Tiny organisms, or animals, that float on the surface of water and feed on phytoplankton

Index

Acknowledgments

Photographs
Tom Stack and Associates:
   Terry Donnelly: page 19 (bottom right)
   G.C. Kelley: page 19
   Thomas Kitchin: page 25 (inset)
   J. Lotter: page 11 (bottom)
   Denise Tackett: page 15
   Robert Winslow: page 13 (inset)
Other photographs by Digital Stock and Digital Vision

Illustrations
Barbara Bedell: pages 4, 5, 6, 8, 9, 14, 19 (left), 20, 21, 22, 24, 26, 27, 28-29, 30
Jeanette McNaughton: page 19 (bottom right)
Halina Below-Spada: page 23